IMAGES
of America

MARLBOROUGH

Meet Me at Marlborough Postcard, 1911. According to the July 17, 1911, *Kingston Daily Freeman*, "Marlborough village is preparing for an Old Home Week celebration the week beginning September 24th. Among the attractions to be offered will be a fruit exhibit, which it is promised will rival anything ever seen in the state. Valuable prizes will be offered for competitors." This postcard was published by J. Ruben of Newburgh, New York. (Courtesy of the Marlboro Free Library.)

On the Cover: A gentlemen and a lady "farmerette" pack up fruit to be shipped to market in Marlborough during World War I. (Courtesy of the Marlboro Free Library.)

Emily Amodeo, Joanne Sagarese Pagnotta,
and James B. Cosgrove for the
Marlboro Free Library

ISBN 978-1-5316-6604-0

Published by Arcadia Publishing
Charleston, South Carolina

Library of Congress Control Number: 2012942685

For all general information, please contact Arcadia Publishing:
Telephone 843-853-2070
Fax 843-853-0044
E-mail sales@arcadiapublishing.com
For customer service and orders:
Toll-Free 1-888-313-2665

Visit us on the Internet at www.arcadiapublishing.com

Emily dedicates this book to her amazing, supportive family and her husband, Stephan. Joanne dedicates this book to the people of Marlboro and Milton, who so generously donated their local historical photographs and artifacts to Marlborough Free Library throughout the years. James dedicates this book to the past and present board and staff members of the Marlboro Free Library, especially Elizabeth S. Manion, who served meritoriously in both capacities.

Contents

Acknowledgments

We would like to send out thanks and appreciation to our editors at Arcadia Publishing, Erin Vosgien and Caitrin Cunningham, for their continued patience and guidance with this project, and also to the former director of the Marlboro Free Library Elizabeth Manion for starting the local history section.

Much thanks to Gerard Mastropaolo for all his help with history questions and for allowing us to use some of his postcards. Unless otherwise noted, the images in this volume appear courtesy of the Marlboro Free Library.

INTRODUCTION

The earliest and most comprehensive histories of Marlborough are Charles Henry Cochrane's 1887 work, *The History of the Town of Marlborough, Ulster County, New York: From the First Settlement in 1712 by Capt. Wm. Bond to 1887*, and C.M. Woolsey's 1908 book, *History of the Town of Marlborough, Ulster County, New York: From its Earliest Discovery*. These histories have been kept in continuous publication through the efforts of the Marlboro-Milton Historical Society and they form the basis for most of what we know about the area's beginnings.

In the 1980s, the Marlboro Free Library, under the directorship of Elizabeth S. Manion, began its local history section, which included a collection of photographs donated by members of the community. Since that time, the growing collection, which forms the majority of images in this book, has been curated by Joanne S. Pagnotta. Library director James Cosgrove, with the assistance of coauthor Emily Amodeo, gave much of the collection worldwide exposure via the Internet. In 2002, the Marlboro Free Library was the first public library to join the Hudson River Valley Heritage website, which features historical photographic collections from organizations in the Hudson Valley. Amodeo began the library's local history blog in 2010, and she continues to maintain and update it. The library celebrated its 100th anniversary on December 9, 2011.

The passage of time has made a few local names somewhat confusing; the reader should keep in mind that the Town of Marlborough consists of three hamlets: Marlboro, Milton, and Lattintown (sometimes seen as Lattingtown). Although the town started as part of Orange County, New York, it has been firmly established in Ulster County since the early 1800s. However, the Marlboro Central School District, which includes the majority of the town, does include a slice of Orange County as well as a small part of the Town of Plattekill.

Marlborough was named for John Churchill (1650–1722), the Duke of Marlborough. The original precinct of New Marlborough officially became a town in 1788. Marlborough is in the southeast corner of Ulster County, halfway between New York City and Albany. Among the early settlers of the town were the Hallock family in Milton, the DuBois family in Marlboro, and the Carpenter family in Lattintown.

Due to its close proximity to the Hudson River and its fertile ground, Marlborough quickly established itself as a farming community. Crops were sent to New York City first by steamboat, later by train, and eventually by truck. In 1912, the Hudson Valley Fruit Exchange was organized to support the farmers. The Whitney Basket Factory, where the Falcon Arts Center is today, once provided baskets for farmers to package fruit for shipping. Raspberries, apples, and grapes continue to be the main crops in Marlborough. According to Woolsey in 1908, "The once famous Antwerp raspberry was the commencement of fruit raising in the town." The production of grapes led to the growth of many local wineries. Most of the town's original family farms are still in business today.

Today, Meet Me in Marlborough is an organized farm trail that celebrates local farming by hosting many events and farm markets through the growing season each year. According to its website,

"This community organization is a group of Milton and Marlboro farmers and businesspeople united to promote local agriculture and tourism to a regional market."

Marlborough also provides a beautiful setting for creativity, with its apple orchards and the surrounding view of the majestic Hudson River. Marlborough has inspired resident and visiting artists throughout the years. Famed turn-of-the-20th-century artist and illustrator Mary Hallock Foote was born and raised in Milton.

Type designer Frederic W. Goudy lived in Marlboro from 1924 until his death in 1947. His home on Old Post Road was called Deepdene. Goudy set up a shop on his property where he designed many font types. In his book, *Goudy's Type Designs: His Story and Specimens*, he wrote, "The type was given the name 'Marlborough' after the name of the town where it was designed. I do not think the town itself was ever aware of the 'honor' paid it!" In his introduction to the book, J. Ben Lieberman wrote, "Frederic W. Goudy . . . was a genius and a giant among type designers, and he ranks with the immortals who altered fundamentally the styles of our typefaces."

John Burroughs (1837–1921), a well-known local author, naturalist, poet, ornithologist, and teacher according to Edward Kanze's *The World of John Burroughs*, taught at Marlboro and in Milton from 1860 to 1863.

Stacy B. Epstein, in an essay in *Alfred H. Maurer: Aestheticism to Modernism*, confirms that Maurer (1869–1932) spent vacations "at the Shady Brook boardinghouse in Marlboro," where he painted many landscape views of the town. In her biography *A.H. Maurer*, Elizabeth McCausland describes him as "the first American pioneer of modern art."

Opera singer Dorothy Maynor (1910–1996) lived at what is now Buttermilk Falls Inn and Spa in Milton. Maynor was the first African American and the first woman to be on the board of the Metropolitan Opera in New York City.

In *History of the Town of Marlborough*, William Plank writes, "James Scott, a Wisconsin lad who came to Milton with the Elverhoj Art Colony in its day, stayed on to become a well known painter, etcher and jewelry maker." In addition, in *The History of Ulster County: With Emphasis upon the Last 100 Years, 1883–1983*, John Matthews wrote, "During the late 1800's and the early 1900's, many summer boarders came to spend vacations in Milton and Marlborough."

In addition to the famous artists who have made Marlborough home, the area has many historical sites and notable businesses. The Friends of the Milton-On-Hudson Train Station have gone to great lengths to restore the 1883 Milton train station back to its original beauty. The Gomez Mill House, established in 1714, is the earliest Jewish homestead in North America. Both are in the National Register of Historic Places.

The Falcon Arts Center building has a long and varied history in Marlboro, having served as a 19th-century button factory, a community center, a basket factory, and a cabinetmaking factory. Amodeo's Sunoco Station, still in business after 66 years, works hard to maintain its allure as a classic American service station. The Raccoon Saloon in the center of Marlboro is one of the oldest and most recognizable buildings in Marlboro and has a spectacular view of the Hudson River from its back balcony.

With a population of 12,688, Marlborough reached its 224th year as an official town in 2012. Although it continues to grow, its small-town charms remain intact.

One

Hamlets of Marlborough

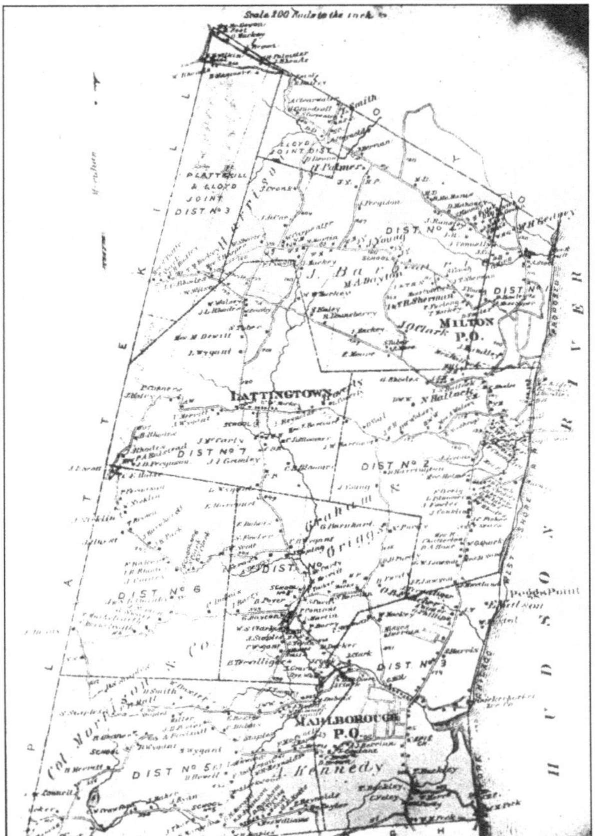

Town Map, 1875. This map of the Town of Marlborough shows the hamlets of Milton, Lattingtown, and Marlboro. In 1900, the town, consisting of 14,300 acres, had a population of 4,000. Most of the names listed as property owners are still common in the area, including Clark, Wygant, Mackey, Rhodes, and Young. (Map by F.W. Beers, from C.M. Woolsey's *The History of the Town of Marlborough.*)

North Main Street, Marlboro. This undated postcard centers on the Hartshorn-Zackary House, the home of local physician Dr. Zackary. A pedestrian walks up what is now Birdsall Avenue from Main Street, commonly known today as State Route 9W. This home features a mansard roof, which came into vogue in American home construction in the early 1870s.

Main Street, Milton. According to William Plank's 1959 history of Marlborough, "Milton had a steady growth during the first half of the 1800s, often leading Marlboro as a center of trade. This was due in part to the large amount of river shipping and its business activity was greatly stimulated by the construction of the turnpike west to Plattekill in 1808." (Courtesy of Joanne Pagnotta.)

1933 POSTCARD OF LATTINTOWN. According to Plank's history, "the leading settlement in Marlborough in the early 1800s was not Marlboro, nor was it Milton, it was Lattintown. It was not only the center of business activity, but of fun and frolic. There was frequently horseracing, often pugilistic encounters, dances and big Fourth of July celebrations when a Revolutionary cannon was fired annually. The hamlet had a harness maker, a hatter, tailor, wagon maker, an undertaker, a tanner and merchants." In his *History of the Town of Marlborough*, Charles Meech Woolsey referred to Lattintown as "the oldest neighborhood or hamlet" in Marlborough. Woolsey went on to describe that in the early 1800s, "there were many large apple orchards in Lattintown," which are still there today. According to Plank, "River commerce took most of the trade to Marlboro and Milton around 1825, and Lattintown became a ghost of its former self." This postcard was published by F. DeMaria of New York City.

Hudson River from Marlboro. Looking east from a hill behind the town, the Presbyterian church stands tall on the corner of West and DuBois Streets. This photograph predates the 1915 Methodist church fire, whose flames engulfed and destroyed that church as well as the wooden spire of this church's steeple.

HUDSON RIVER FROM MILTON. This view is from the Kent family farm, which is still operational today. Hudson River towns were prime spots for transportation, factories, farming, and commerce. According to Plank, "Crate factories were in operation in Milton for many years." This postcard, published by W.A. Goehringer, was donated by Fred Woolsey.

Two

TRANSPORTATION

MARY POWELL STEAMBOAT. According to Plank, "About 1805, Thomas Powell, prominent ship owner of Newburgh, was attracted to Milton by the increasing commerce it enjoyed, and built a dock. His wife was Mary Powell, whose name was given to the fastest and famous steamer on the Hudson. The *Mary Powell* made regular stops at Milton on her Rondout–New York run for over half a century."

Tug at Marlboro Dock. The tugboat *Edwin H. Mead* was launched by the Cornell Steamboat Company on May 28, 1892, in Newburgh according to a *New York Times* article. The article described the tugboat as being "120 feet long and having a 25 foot beam." This photograph was taken by Ralph P. Young at the Marlboro Ice House dock around 1908 and is now part of the DuBois Collection in the library archives.

The *Benjamin B. O'Dell*. Benjamin Barker O'Dell Sr. (1825–1916) was the mayor of Newburgh and the head of the Central Hudson Steamboat Company. Here, the steamboat bearing his name, which was built in 1910, passes Young's Dock at Marlboro on June 22, 1916. This photograph was also taken by Ralph P. Young and is in the Dubois Collection.

CREW AND PASSENGERS ON THE *BENJAMIN B. O'DELL*. Posing on the steamboat are, from left to right, (first row) Jesse Travis, second pilot; Sam Crum, general manager; George B. Greenwood, first pilot; Fred Simpson, captain; Herbert O'Dell, son of Benjamin O'Dell Sr.; Arthur Palmer, purser; and Charles Kotch, first mate from Kingston. Standing on the stairs behind Simpson is Benjamin B. O'Dell Jr., former governor of New York; behind him is Benjamin B. O'Dell Sr., former mayor of Newburgh; at the top of the stairs is Scott Corwin, general freight agent. According to an April 1, 1911, *New York Times* article titled "New River Steamer Coming," the *Benjamin B. O'Dell* was "more like an Atlantic steamship than a river steamer. She was 280 feet long, 50 feet extreme breadth, and [had] a speed of 18 knots. She would carry 400 tons of freight." This photograph is in the library's Badner Collection.

Marlboro Railroad Station. In his 1908 history of the town, Charles Woolsey wrote that "the West Shore Railroad has been of great benefit; most of the trains stop at Milton and Marlborough; it furnished refrigerator cars and ships fruit wherever desired." This station was known as the "upper station" to locals at the time.

Badner Band at Marlboro Station. According to *Picture Book, As We Were—As We Are*, "George Badner's band is shown here at the Marlboro Station awaiting the arrival of celebrities. The old station stood between the railroad tracks and the river. After several tragic accidents, this building was torn down, and a new station was built on the other sides of the tracks."

West Shore Railroad, Marlboro. According to *Picture Book, As We Were—As We Are*, this postcard shows "the last West Shore Railroad station in Marlborough, 1946, which was torn down and used for the building of a home on Mount Zion Road." The railroad shanty in the background "was later moved to the Cluett Schantz home." The postcard is in the library's Badner Collection.

W. S. R. R. STATION, MILTON ON HUDSON, N. Y.

Milton Train Station. This station was established in 1883 for the New York, West Shore & Buffalo Railway. According to an informational pamphlet published by Friends of the Milton-On-Hudson Train Station, the station "was designed by the prominent Philadelphia Architects Wilson Brothers and Company." This postcard is postmarked July 22, 1927, and was published by the Kingston Souvenir Company of New York City. The Milton train station is now in the National Registry of Historic Places. (Courtesy of Gerard M. Mastropaolo.)

McMULLEN'S TAXI, MARLBORO. The early-1900s taxi above was most likely used by guests at Moses McMullen's Inn. Today, the Raccoon Saloon occupies the former inn on Route 9W. According to his obituary in the July 3, 1930, *New York Times*, in addition to operating the inn for a half-century, McMullen was also a "well-known horseman." This photograph is from the DuBois Collection.

EARLY AUTOMOBILE, MARLBORO. The label on the back of this photograph states that this vehicle was purchased with cigar bands by Edward McGowan. The riders are identified as Jim McGowan and Frank Shore. Judging by the flags on the building, this picture was most likely taken during the town's 1911 Old Home Week celebration. The photograph is part of the Mannese/Panzella Collection.

Three

Farming and Wineries

Kaley Farm. Before the introduction of the tractor, horses were the main means of power on the farms of Marlborough. This 1913 photograph shows an Irish draft horse on the Kaley farm on Willow Tree Road in Milton. An early version of a speed-sprayer is behind the horse and the unidentified farmhand. (Courtesy of Joanne Pagnotta.)

PIZZO FARM. Horses were used on some farms well into the 1950s. This photograph, taken on the Pizzo farm on April 10, 1950, is labeled "first day driving posts." John Pizzo is on the wagon with the maul, and the others are identified by John Pizzo as Patrick Corrado and James Festa. (Courtesy of John Pizzo.)

YOUNG'S FARM. According to Cochrane, "In 1858, William Young bought property in Marlboro, where he established a fruit farm." Part of the farm was on the east side of Route 9W on the current site of Marlboro Elementary School. In this photograph from the Badner Collection, a farmer plows the field with a team of horses.

YOUNG'S GRAPE VINEYARDS. This vineyard was located on the west side of Route 9W north of the current Marlboro Middle School near Purdy Avenue. In the distance on the left are the barns of Col. Lewis DuBois, who established his home there prior to 1770. The vineyard now belongs to the Rusk family. This photograph is from the Badner Collection.

CAMP YOUNG. This farm camp was on the west side of Route 9W, north of the current site of Marlboro Middle School. It housed young people who volunteered to work on the farms during World War I. Extra hands were recruited to tend and harvest crops because many local laborers were away in military service. This photograph is also from the Badner Collection.

World War I Farmerettes. From 1917 to 1919, the Woman's Land Army of America, also known as the Farmerettes, came to Marlborough to work on the farms while the young men were away serving in the Armed Forces. According to a May 29, 2009, *Smithsonian* article titled "Before Rosie the Riveter, Farmerettes Went to Work," "the farmerettes were shocking at first—wearing pants!—but farmers began to rely upon the women workers."

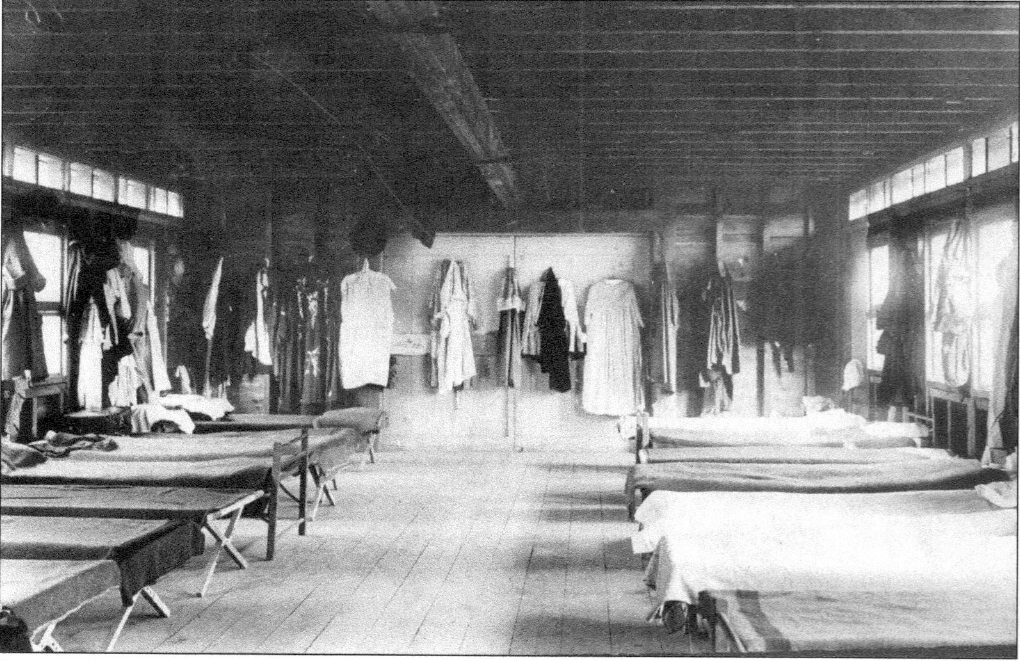

Interior of Camp Young Dormitory. Farmerettes lived in dormitory-style buildings like this one on the Young farm. The interior appears to be spacious and well ventilated, providing each lady with a cot and clothing hooks.

Farmerette Picking Currants. The Caywood variety of currants was developed in 1884 by A.J. Caywood. The Caywood farm, on Old Post Road, was later known as Shady Brook Farms and is currently owned by Maurice and Mary Menasche.

Early Italian Immigrant Farmers. Five-year-old Thomas LaPolla (seated far left) takes a break from picking strawberries with his family in 1910. The LaPolla family came to the United States in 1893, originally settling in New York City and then moving to Milton in the early 1900s. (Courtesy of JoAnne Pagnotta.)

Farming during World War I. Every year in the late summer, the local fruit was picked by both men and women and then sorted and placed in large crates. The crates, filled with pears, apples, peaches, and grapes, were moved from local farms by horse and wagon to Young's Dock in Marlboro and Sands Dock in Milton, where they were shipped to New York City by steamboats.

Packing and Transporting Fruit during World War I. Packaged fruit is unloaded at the dock storage area and awaits shipment to New York City. Sailing sloops were replaced by steamboats as the fastest way to ship produce to New York City. After the New York, West Shore & Buffalo Railway line was completed in 1883, it replaced steamboats as the main means of transporting produce to market.

Fruit Blossoms, Marlborough. Spring is beautiful in Marlborough, as cherry, peach, and pear trees fill the Hudson Valley with white and pink blossoms. These apple trees on the banks of the Hudson River exemplify the predominance of apples as a cash harvest since the early 1900s.

Harvesting Fruit. Apple pickers follow a tractor dropping large fruit bins strategically throughout the orchard. In the 1800s, Irish and Italian immigrants made up the corps of seasonal workers coming to Marlborough to harvest and pack fruit in the fall. Most of today's temporary workers are of Jamaican and Mexican heritage. Many Marlborough farms have also embraced the "pick your own" concept for visiting tourists and locals alike.

Locust Grove Fruit Farm, Milton. Barns were used to sort and pack the fruit and house the farm animals and equipment. This barn complex was on the Kent family property on old Route 9W. The Kents still operate a seventh-generation family farm there. These barns were built by Charles Conklin in 1877 and were destroyed in a 1989 fire.

Quimby Barns, Mount Zion Road, Marlboro. According to *Picture Book, As We Were—As We Are*, from which this 1978 photograph is taken, "James Clark came to America from Northern Ireland in the 1700s and acquired this land." According to the present owners, Howard and Phoebe Quimby, the first of these barns was constructed in the mid- to late 1700s and has been in continuous use since.

Royal Kedem Winery. The Kedem Winery was originally located at the foot of Dock Road in Milton on the shore of the Hudson River. The building was originally part of the Hudson Valley Fruit Exchange, which then operated as a cold storage until it was sold to the Kedem Winery in 1948. Royal Kedem Winery is now located on Route 9W in Marlboro. According to the Spring 2010 issue of *Hudson Valley Wine*, Royal Kedem Winery "is the leader now in the Kosher beverage industry, and imports foods from around the world." (Both, from Royal Kedem Winery brochure.)

Mark Miller Map of Benmarl Vineyards, 1976. According to a June 12, 1987, article in the *Evening News* titled "Benmarl Vineyard Oldest in Country," "Benmarl is the oldest continuously operated vineyard in the United States. The vineyard was founded in the mid-18th century by A.J. Caywood, the grandfather of William Wardell and purchased by Mark Miller in 1956. Benmarl Winery received the first farm producer license in 1976, allowing sale of wine from the small retail store on location." Benmarl wine can be found in many retail outlets throughout the country. The land surrounding the winery has had vineyards on it since the 1800s. Over the past decade, several other wineries came into being in Marlborough. Glorie Farm Winery is housed in a 1913 barn on Mountain Road. Stoutridge Vineyards is on Ann Kaley Lane. All local wineries are now part of the Shawangunk Wine Trail.

Four

Churches

Chapel Hill Community Church. This historic church is on Bingham Road in Marlboro. In an August 17, 2011, *Poughkeepsie Journal* article, Anthony P. Musso writes, "It was built in 1860 as a chapel for the Amity Baptist Church on 54th Street in New York City." In 1905, preacher Leighton Williams "had the chapel disassembled, transported to his property in Marlboro, and rebuilt at its current location."

Christ Episcopal Church, Marlboro. This congregation began in Marlboro in 1836. The church building, which still stands, was erected in 1858, making it the third Episcopal church founded in Ulster County. Trinity Church, in the village of Ulster, was the first, beginning in 1831, and St. John's, in Kingston, was the second, starting in 1833.

Baptist Church, Lattintown. This congregation was officially incorporated on January 26, 1807, although, according to Plank, "Meetings for members of the Baptist Church were first held in the Lattintown School building in 1789." The church building was erected in June 1810. The building now houses the Mount Carmel Community Church and is in the National Register of Historic Places.

METHODIST EPISCOPAL CHURCH, MARLBORO. This 1892 photograph shows the Methodist Episcopal church that once sat on Grand Street between Dubois and Church Streets. The Methodist church in Marlboro was incorporated on October 28, 1830, and this church was built in 1867 at a cost of $16,000.

INTERIOR OF METHODIST CHURCH, MARLBORO. This church was destroyed by fire in 1915 and rebuilt on the same site. The Methodist church in Milton currently serves as the church for both Marlboro and Milton. The postcard below of the original church was donated by Joan Diorio.

METHODIST EPISCOPAL CHURCH, MILTON. This church, which still stands today, was the first Methodist church in the county, incorporated on November 16, 1812, and built at a cost of $1,907.92. According to Woolsey, "In 1904 and 1905, the church was enlarged and remodeled at an expense of $7,000." This postcard, postmarked May 29, 1905, was donated by Frederic Woolsey.

UNITED PRESBYTERIAN CHURCH, MILTON. According to Woolsey, this church society was "incorporated on August 23, 1841, but early records of the church were lost in an 1843 fire." The original church, on the corner of Main and Church Streets, burned down and was replaced by this church in 1899. (From *Picture Book, As We Were—As We Are.*)

First Presbyterian Church, Marlboro. According to Plank, in 1874, "Reverend Charles Cooper dedicated the new $35,000 brick church on a new site on Grand Street given by Nathaniel DuBois. It was debt free." The previous church, destroyed in an 1869 fire, was on Route 9W, where its churchyard remains next to Riverside Cemetery. The church, facing the corner of West and DuBois Streets, still stands today.

The Women's Missionary Society. In this undated photograph, members pose on the front lawn of the First Presbyterian Church in Marlboro. According to Plank, "In 1884–1892, Reverend Charles Bronson helped with the formation of the Missionary, and from 1892–1899, Reverend Charles Carhart greatly developed the Missionary work."

St. James Catholic Church and Rectory, Milton-on-Hudson, N. Y.

ST. JAMES ROMAN CATHOLIC CHURCH, MILTON. According to Woolsey, in 1874, "Reverend James Francis Mee was appointed pastor of the Milton parish. He was the first resident pastor of Milton. There was not a Catholic Church then, but a house for a parochial residence had already been secured by the parishioners. In 1876, the Milton church [above] was completed."

Our Lady of Mercy Church
Roseton, New York

OUR LADY OF MERCY ROMAN CATHOLIC CHURCH, ROSETON. According to the timeline in *St. Mary's 100 Years Celebration* yearbook, compiled in 2000 by Elizabeth S. Manion, Juan J. and Marie Jova, owners of the Jova Brick Yards in Roseton, built Our Lady of Mercy Church (left) in Roseton, where services are still held. In 1900, Our Lady of Mercy became a joint parish with St. Mary's Church in Marlboro.

St. Mary's Roman Catholic Church, Marlboro. According to the *St. Mary's 100 Years Celebration* yearbook, "This church was legally incorporated as a parish on January 3, 1900. From as early as 1865 though, mass was celebrated in Marlboro every two of three weeks at the Pleasant View Hotel, or in private homes. The old Methodist Meeting House, which was where States Sarles and Son was located on Route 9W, was once used for Catholic Church services. In 1922, the cornerstone for Saint Mary's Church on Route 9W was laid, and Mrs. Marie Jova donated all the exterior bricks. In 1924, the main marble altar was consecrated on April 27th by Bishop John J. Dunn, and the new Saint Mary's Church was officially dedicated."

Society of Friends, Milton. According to Woolsey, "In the year 1789, the Cornwall monthly meeting authorized William Thorn, Jacob Wright, Edward Hallock and Alexander Young, as trustees, to purchase from Daniel Knowlton seven acres of land one mile south of Milton and on the west side of the main road opposite to the house where Edward Hallock had held his first meetings. This was the first purchase of land for church purposes by the Friends in Ulster County. During the Civil War, several Quakers from Milton served in the army. For years before the Civil War, the Quakers had been opposed to slavery, and it was claimed that there were stations among them where the slave escaping from bondage could find a safe refuge and be helped on his/her journey to freedom." This view from the church shows the village of Milton.

Five

LOCAL BUSINESSES

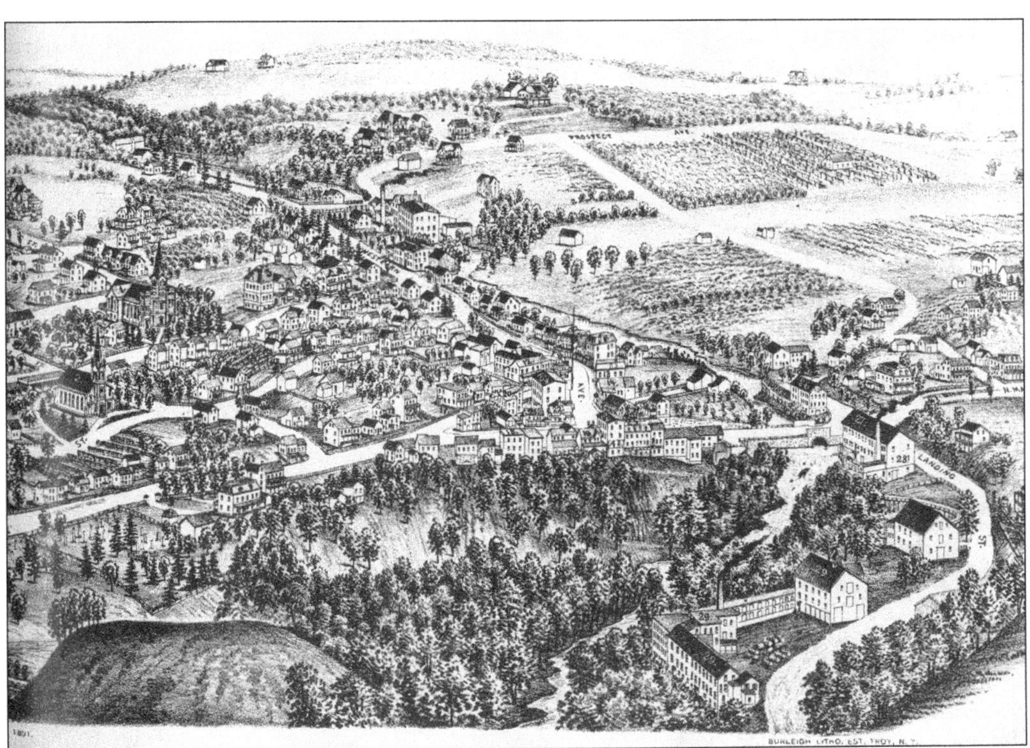

PANORAMIC MAP OF MARLBORO VILLAGE. This 1891 lithograph created and sold by the L.R. Burleigh Company of Troy, New York, shows the residences and businesses of Marlboro, such as the Pleasant View Hotel, the office of Dr. Albert Palmer, and the Marlborough Record Office. The map was republished locally by Henry Schlesinger in 1976 in celebration of the national bicentennial.

First National Bank of Marlborough. According to Woolsey, "This bank was organized in August 1907, with a capital of $25,000." Woolsey also writes, "The village was incorporated in July 1906. The population was about 800." The bank faced Route 9W at the corner of Western Avenue, the current site of KeyBank. This postcard is from the Badner Collection.

Interior of First National Bank of Marlborough. According to Plank, "C.W. Davis of Atlanta, Georgia was the first cashier, followed by W. P. Garmany, another Georgian, who settled here and became a prominent fruit grower. Edmund Carpenter became cashier after entering the business in 1911." This postcard was published by the Kingston Souvenir Company. (Courtesy of Dennis and Pamela McCourt.)

First National Bank, Milton. According to Plank, "This bank was organized on March 19, 1920 with R.M. Rownd as president, J.J. Kaley as vice-president, and a board of directors composed of these two with J.A. Driscoll, John Ball, Percy Bunker, E.F. Carpenter, R.W. Hallock, Charles Mataraza and J.R. Clark. Originally, the capital was $25,000." The bank later became the First National Bank of Highland. (From *Picture Book, As We Were—As We Are.*)

Kaley Store, Milton. The popular general goods store below, at the corner of Main Street and Milton Turnpike, was owned by Joseph J. Kaley from 1892 to 1931. According to a November 13, 1931, *Milton Messenger* newspaper article titled "Famous Old Store Has Been Sold," this building was once a "drug store, doctors office, telegraph office, a meat market, coal and lumber business, grocery and general store." (Courtesy of Joanne Pagnotta.)

BELL'S MILL, MILTON. This factory operated from the late 1800s until about 1910. According to John Matthews in *The History of Ulster County*, Bell's Mill "was located on the site of the Kedem Winery's main building" at the foot of Dock Road and manufactured "eiderdown and woolen material." Matthews also wrote, "In the early 1920s, Walter MacMichael reopened Bell's Factory under the name of the Milton Woolen Mills."

WHITNEY BASKET FACTORY, DOCK ROAD, MARLBORO. According to Plank, the Whitney Basket factory, seen here, "was the largest manufacturing establishment the town has ever had, beginning in 1853 when John F. Whitney began making packages to serve the growing fruit industry." This photograph is from the Badner Collection.

Pleasant View Hotel, Marlboro. Pictured in 1911, the Pleasant View Hotel, also known as the McMullen House, was on Route 9W. It was owned by two generations of the McMullen family from 1862 to 1930. In later years, under the ownership of Gus Mondello, it was called the Riverview Hotel. It is now the Raccoon Saloon.

Sucker Hole, Marlboro. At the bottom of this drop that extends from behind the current Amodeo Bros. Service Station to the Raccoon Saloon on Route 9W is a pond popularly known as the sucker hole because of the many suckerfish caught from it. An 1886 *New York Times* article titled "Fell Over a Precipice" reports the death of " 'Buffalo Frank' [who] fell to the bottom of the 'sucker hole' after losing his footing at the rear of the McMullen House."

Post Office, Marlboro. Regular mail service was established in Marlboro in 1824. This early location of the US post office was on Western Avenue in the Carpenter Building in the center of the village.

Marlboro Post Office Dedication. The new post office on Western Avenue was dedicated on September 20, 1958. Addressing fellow citizens from the podium is Gus J. Cutrone, who served as postmaster from 1954 to 1984. Frank Iannella served as postmaster from 1993 to 2009. This photograph was donated by John J. Cutrone.

MERRITT'S STORE, 1911. John Carlton Merritt was born in the village of Marlboro on July 18, 1884, to Edward A. and Emeline Kniffin Merritt. He went on to open this grocery store on Western Avenue in 1875. This photograph is from the DuBois Collection.

HARTSHORN BUILDING, MARLBORO. Prior to 1897, Samuel Corwin's Sons dry goods occupied the first floor of this building. Charles A. Hartshorn owned this building, which still stands on the east side of Route 9W, from the early 1900s, when it housed a general store. At that time, the *Marlborough Record* office occupied the second floor. The third floor was once a meeting place for the Advance Lodge of Odd Fellows. Among the many businesses in the building between the 1930s and the 1950s were a movie theater and a barbershop. Presently, the ground floor is occupied by Pizza Town, and the upper floors have been converted into living quarters.

Button Factory, Marlboro. This building at 1348 Route 9W, which now houses the Falcon Arts Center, "was once a 19th-century button factory, power generated by the small, scenic waterfall over which the building is still perched," according to a February 10, 2011, *Hudson Valley Times* article by Frances Marion Platt titled "Flight of the Falcon." The building was also once known as the Rink Building because of the roller rink located inside in the 1880s and 1890s. According to Plank, "There have been mills on this site, such as the Grist Wright's Feed Mill. In 1885, the *Marlborough Progress*, a four-page newspaper was started on the second floor by Charles H. Cochrane and M.F. Applegate. This building also served as a place for political gatherings and dances during the 1920s." Today, it is owned by the Falco family.

DEXTER'S DEPARTMENT STORE, MARLBORO. Before this building housed Dexter's, it was Samuel Corwin's Sons dry goods store in 1891. In this photograph, it is decorated for the 1911 Old Home Week. Today, the parking lot for the Pizza Town restaurant occupies this spot.

EXCHANGE HOTEL, MARLBORO. This early-1900s hotel was on King Street near the current location of Cibo's Restaurant. Jason McGowan was the hotelkeeper. The fire hydrant and public water trough in the foreground indicate the importance of the King Street and Western Avenue intersection as the center of the village. The flagpole/hydrant configuration was moved slightly north of this location, but it remains a benchmark of the village center.

TOMATO CANNING FACTORY, MARLBORO. The original investors in the canning factory gathered together in 1933 on Western Avenue for this photograph. The investors included, from left to right, (first row) attorney Henry Palermo, Steve Zambito, Antonino Canzoneri, Tony Canzoneri Jr., Salvatore Zambito, Joseph Pizzo, John Antinoti, Ignazio Zambito, Ignazio Dina, and unidentified; (second row) Giuseppe Garcia, Chet Yeaples, Alphonso Favata, Tony Lopresti, Manel Lopez, Joe Favata, Howard Baker Sr., Joe Zambito, Andrew Berkery, Victor Lata, Nicholas Mertes, John Downer, Ed McGowan, Ignazio Comporetto, Domenico Chillura, and Onofrio "Frank" Zambito. The photograph was taken by professional photographer Augusto Galati of Newburgh. At one time, this building was also a cider mill. (Courtesy of Dr. Anthony M. Pascale.)

Marlboro Hardware Store, 1896. This photograph shows the preparations that were made to move this store to its new site on Route 9W, north of Western Avenue. The building still exists today and is owned by the Kronner family, but it is no longer a hardware store. According to the Marlboro publication *Picture Book, As We Were—As We Are*, this store and home originally "stood at the corner of Route 9W and Western Avenue [as early as] 1830. John Badner, an emigrant from Germany, kept a store and shoe shop there. In 1895, he took off a west lean-to and raised it up to be the 2nd and 3rd stories, front only of the building. George Badner put the apartment over a saloon, with the old house on top. [Later, the building] was sold to Leo Kronner." This photograph is from the Badner Collection.

Samuel Corwin's Sons, Marlboro. This store sold dry goods and fancy groceries. It also shared space with a satellite office of the *Kingston Freeman*, which is still in publication. The Ketcham Post Band No. 495 of Marlborough poses here for Decoration Day, May 30, 1889. Ed McCarthy is listed on the back as one of the band members. This photograph is from the Badner Collection.

Badner Shoe Shop, Marlboro. This building is believed to be the home and business of German immigrant John Badner, who lived there as early as 1830. His shop was at 4 Western Avenue, the current location of Frank's Deli, near the corner of Route 9W. The gentleman seen here may be Badner's son, George, who added a general store to the original business.

B. HERBERICH BAKERY, MARLBORO. The Herberich family poses proudly in front of their Western Avenue shop in 1913. They are, from left to right, Ludwig Herberich; Barney Herberich; Max, the baker; Ella Zierger; and Albertina Zimmerman. The photograph was donated by Virginia Herberich McCourt.

MARLBORO STOREFRONT. Noting the proliferation of flags and patriotic bunting in this photograph, it was most likely taken during one of the Old Home Weeks in the early 1900s. The Salada Tea Company was founded in 1892. This photograph is from the Badner Collection.

MARLBOROUGH GARAGE, MARLBORO. The distinctive roofline of this building can still be recognized over what is now the River Depot shops and apartments on Route 9W just south of the Amodeo Bros. Service Station. In the past, it was a bus garage. This postcard, published by the Ess and Ess Photograph Company in New York City, was donated by Joan Diorio.

SHIP LANTERN INN, MILTON. This restaurant, at 1725 Route 9W, has been in continuous operation since 1925. According to its website, "John Foglia's Ship Lantern Inn on Route 9W is the oldest restaurant in the valley serving continental food. The building dates back to Revolutionary War days. Mr. Foglia is one of the four original founders of the renowned Chef-Boy-Ar-Dee Company." This postcard was published by Henry Reichert of Poughkeepsie.

Young's Dock, Marlboro. Young's dock stood directly on the shore of the Hudson River on Dock Road, on the present site of the Marlboro Yacht Club. Fruit crops, among other commodities, were shipped to New York City from Marlboro regularly from here. This early-1900s photograph is from the DuBois Collection.

Warren Blacksmith Shop, Marlboro. This blacksmith shop, on Western Avenue, pictured in the early 1900s, later became a winery in the 1950s. Decker's blacksmith shop on Route 9W in Marlboro was another local blacksmith shop at the time. This photograph originally belonged to Ethelyn Rich and was donated to the library by John Badner.

Six

LIBRARIES

MILTON LIBRARY. When Sarah Hull Hallock died in 1884, she left an endowment to maintain a free library in the village of Milton. Shortly afterward, trustees were appointed and the library came into being. According to Plank, "From 1896 until about 1924, the library was housed in the Woolsey Building on Main Street."

Sarah Hull Hallock. Sarah Hull Hallock was born to a Quaker family in Milton in the 1800s and, according to Foote, "was far ahead of all the men and most of the women of [her] family on the question of Women's Rights. She also belonged to the New York Anti-Slavery Society." (Courtesy of the Sarah Hull Hallock Free Library.)

Sarah Hull Hallock Free Library, Milton. From 1920 to 1924, thanks to the efforts of the library trustees, the Maids and Matrons Society, and other community members, land was purchased and construction began on the Sarah Hull Hallock Free Library. To meet the growing population, the library building was expanded in 1989.

Hallock Library Expansion, Milton. In 1989, through the generosity of Roy Featherstone, an anonymous challenge grant, and a New York State grant, the library (above) was enlarged to its present size. Viewed here from Main Street, the expanded edifice gives the impression of twin buildings, but it is actually one building. The library was built into a hill, making the first story accessible from Dock Road. In 2011, the library was again upgraded with a Main Street grant from the state. (Courtesy of Linda LaPolla.)

Marlboro Free Library. On December 9, 1911, Marlboro was granted a provisional charter for a public library by the New York State Board of Regents. Library service began in the Marlboro Union Free School at the corner of Grand and Church Streets and then moved to the basement of the Methodist Episcopal church. Library materials were lost when the church burned down in 1914. This photograph was donated by Frederick Woolsey.

Marlboro Free Library, King Street, Marlboro. According to Plank, "Largely through the earnest work of Ralph Young in raising money, the new library at the corner of King Street and Route 9W opened in 1921." In 1959, the Marlborough Free Library joined the newly formed Mid-Hudson Library System, a cooperative library system developed to assist local libraries in upgrading service. In 1970, Flossie Linsig retired as Marlboro librarian after 20 years of service to the community. In 1972, the status of the library was changed from an association library to a school district public library. In 1977, it was determined by the board of trustees that the village was in need of a larger library. This postcard was published by A. Biren of Brooklyn, New York.

Marlboro Free Library, Route 9W, Marlboro. The building set back at the corner of Bloom Street and Route 9W was once a school where the famous American naturalist John Burroughs taught during his early years as an itinerant instructor, from 1860 to 1862. It was torn down in 1957 and is now the location of the Marlboro Free Library. The Rusk family donated the land to the library board. Neither building shown still exists.

Marlboro Free Library Fair. Jacqueline Conn (left) and Elizabeth Manion prepare sale items to raise funds for the construction of the new library. A library fair was held each summer. Manion, who was a library trustee at the time, subsequently earned her master's of library science degree and served as director of the library from 1985 until her retirement in 2002.

MARLBORO LIBRARY CONSTRUCTION. Milton Chazen Associates designed the new, 3,600-square-foot Marlboro Free Library building at the corner of Route 9W and Bloom Street in 1977. Bids for construction of the new library and the sale of the King Street building were published in the *Southern Ulster Pioneer* and the *Evening News* on May 11 of that year. Bids were opened on May 27, and contracts were awarded on July 11. The library was completed one year later, and the dedication took place on May 21, 1978. This library is located at 1251 Route 9W and is still home to the Marlboro Free Library. This photograph was taken by Vincent A. Guariylia of Starship Studios.

Marlboro Library Expansion. In 1986, Peter R. Hoffmann of Marlboro was hired as the architect of record to develop plans for an expansion to the library. The positive vote of school district taxpayers on December 18 of that year assured funds for the completion of the project. Formal construction bids for the library expansion were opened on February 6, 1987, and were awarded on March 23. Ground-breaking ceremonies took place on March 25. The dedication ceremonies for the addition took place exactly 10 years to the day after the original dedication of the site. December 9, 2011, marked the 100th anniversary of the library.

ALICE PIERCE HOUSE, MARLBORO. Over the years, the Marlboro Free Library has been the recipient of generous donations. The Pierce family estate enabled the library to purchase land for the future expansion of the library. Dedication of the West Street parking lot and the adjacent property took place at special ceremonies held on Sunday, November 13, 1994.

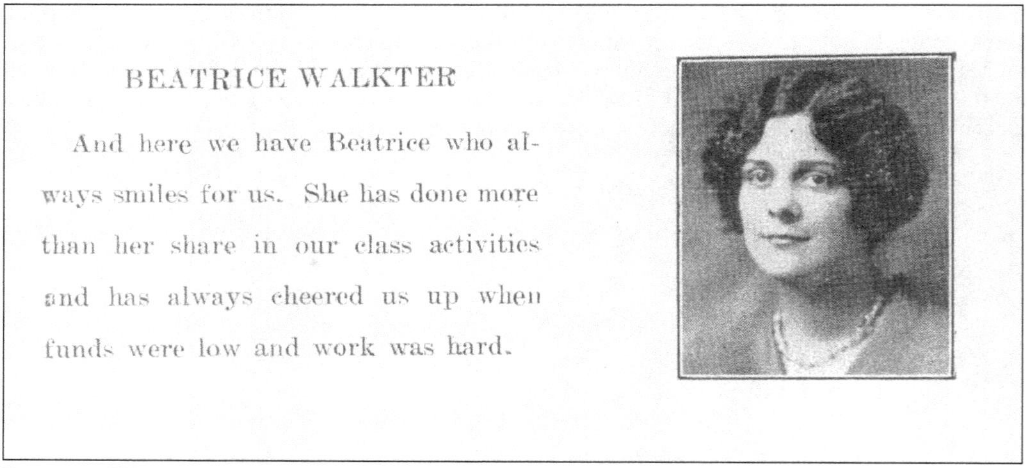

BEATRICE WALKTER

And here we have Beatrice who always smiles for us. She has done more than her share in our class activities and has always cheered us up when funds were low and work was hard.

BEATRICE WALKTER CONOVER. Beatrice Walkter graduated from Marlboro High School in 1929 and married Murray Conover in 1935. Remembering her roots in Marlboro, her family has made numerous generous donations to the Marlboro Free Library. She passed away in August 18, 2009. In 2011, the board of trustees voted that when the library next expands, the local history room will be named after her.

Seven

Marlborough Schools

Aluminum and Tin Collection. This group of Milton classmates worked together to collect donations for the World War II effort at the Milton Elementary School. They are, from left to right, Sam Scilla, Gloria Pesavento, Helen Nantz, and Harvey Christofferson. This photograph is from the Dalby/Lyons Collection.

Lattingtown School. Bertie Clark states in the PTA publication *Schools of the Town of Marlborough*, "The Lattingtown District (No. 7) in 1877 built a new school replacing what appears to have been the original building. The old school had hand-made benches. The large teacher's desk had a door in it. This made a convenient place to stow an unruly pupil, so the story goes. The original school faced the road. The new one-room school was built by Mr. Bloomer, the trustee, who was paid by the district for his labor. This school had seats to replace the old benches. A program of improvements consisting of a furnace driven well, single seats, ventilating system, and an addition, during the trusteeship of James Conklin, Leighton Craft, H.V. Mackey, and Mr. and Mrs. Edgar M. Clarke, Jr., began in 1919 with the painting of the building when Arnold A. Mackey was trustee. These improvements were labeled; "temporary" by the Department of Education at Albany, but the glimpse of modern education it afforded was appreciated by the community."

EARLY PRIVATE SCHOOL, MARLBORO. According to *Schools of the Town of Marlborough*, "For many years the only schools in the Village of Marlborough were private schools and seminaries. One of earliest schools of which we have any record was a boarding and day school kept about 1840 in the old Hepworth brick house, owned by C.S. McCourt, by a gentleman named Northrip. His assistant and oldest daughter became the wife of the Reverend Mr. Clark, a Presbyterian minister, and during the 1860s and 1870s, they conducted a similar academy on the banks of the Hudson at Milton. About 1860–1862, John Burroughs, the great Naturalist of West Park, conducted a private school in this wing of the McCourt home, also. Later, it is thought, Mr. Burroughs taught in the old building that once stood where the present day Marlboro Free Library stands."

RIVERSIDE

Seminary for Young Ladies,

MILTON, ULSTER CO., N. Y.

REV. EDGAR W. CLARKE, A. M.

PROPRIETOR AND PRINCIPAL.

1866–1867.

Poughkeepsie:

ISAAC PLATT & SON, STEAM PRINTERS, DAILY EAGLE OFFICE,

1867.

RIVERSIDE ACADEMY, MILTON. According to Woolsey, "In 1862 the Revered Edgar W. Clark and wife opened a day and boarding school; it was very successful for several years, young ladies attending from most all of the states in the Union. With Mr. Clark's health failing, they moved west, and Mrs. Scofield Brown became the owner. The academy buildings were soon after burned."

MARLBORO UNION FREE SCHOOL CLASSROOM. The seventh-grade class at Marlboro Union Free School on Grand Street poses below in their classroom in 1904. The teachers are Miss Keller and Reuben A. Mabie. Each student signed his or her name on the back of the photograph, which was donated by John Pizzo.

The Marlboro Union Free School. According to *Schools of the Town of Marlborough*, "In 1888, because of crowded conditions, the community strongly felt the need of a new school. After careful deliberation, the property on the northeast corner of Grand and Church Streets was purchased from Matthew Berean." The school was "first opened in December of 1888 with suitable ceremonies in the Principal's room, into which has crowded 160 pupils and visitors." The Marlboro Union Free School was located where the Marlboro Fire House stands today. The Marlboro Free Library began in this school, occupying it from 1911 to 1913 before relocating back again after the Methodist church fire of 1915. By 1936, the building was no longer used as a school, and it became the Hudson River Fruit Exchange. This postcard was published by J. Ruben of Newburgh.

Sands Avenue School, Milton. According to *Schools of the Town of Marlborough*, "The center room was the original one-room school built in 1840. This school with a small hall for the boys and one for the girls contained about 150 desks. A long platform ran the length of the school and on it the pupils stood when reciting. A large round wood stove was in the center of the school room."

Milton Schoolchildren. Schoolchildren gather outside the school located on Shanghai Hill where Sands Avenue meets Dock Road. According to MaryLou Mahan's book, *Marlborough On My Mind*, "the Sands Avenue School served the community from 1840 to 1938."

South Road School, Milton. According to *Schools of the Town of Marlborough*, this school "was built on property secured by deed in 1845 from Nathaniel Hallock." Listed on the back of the photograph are the following names, from left to right: (first row) John Jacob, Martain Daintine, Marie LaGrity, Dorothy Conn, Mildred Conklin, Earl Conklin, Minnie Candita, unidentified, Tony Calbrine, Lessie Labitiz, Joseph Mosley, Helen Mosley, Jack Conn, Ralph Diorio, Dominick Mannese, and Frederick Woolsey; (second row) teacher Miss McManus, Thompson Rounds, Ruth Sears, Lillian Broure, Fannie Romaner, Fannie Calbrine, Luala Olden, Bertha Magyars, Daniel Diorio, Albert Clark, Adeline Sears, Daniel Kovatch, John Kenidith, Patsie Mannese, unidentified, and teacher Miss Palmateer; (third row) Edgar Rhodes, Ida Coch, Mildred Clappy, Anna Coon, Thomes Jinkins, Violet Quick, Katherine McDonald, Francis McCloolin, Bareth McNickolous, Arthur D. Noline, David Conn, Joseph Kovatch, Fred J. Kenney, Rosmond Woolsey, Irene Concline, and Tony Calbrine. (Courtesy of Gerard Mastropaolo.)

Milton Turnpike School. According to *Schools of the Town of Marlborough*, "In 1890, the interior [of this school] was improved with new type desks instead of the original benches. The schoolhouse was built about 1859. The second Turnpike School, familiarly known as Rocky Hill Seminary, [was] the only one built on the site belonging to Hallock Young." This class photograph from 1913 includes, from left to right, (first row) Anna Fox, Sophie Gersch, Helen Taber, Jean Dirago, John Donovan, Millie Dirago, Mary Russo, Catherine Casaburo, Antoinette Dirago, Elizabeth Salzano, Loretta Donovan, Mike Grandios, and Josephine Perrine; (second row) Jerry Casaburo, Rose Dirago, Jim Dirago, Eber Atkins, Wilbur Atkins, Bill Shay, Rocky Grandio, Oscar George Wendover, Joseph Dirago, Ambrose McManus, teacher Miss Perrine, Helen Connors, Mary Casaburo, Mary McManus, and ? Bullet; (third row) Ellen Gersch, Al Taber, Whalen McManus, Joseph Matthews, Edward Young, Angelina Dirago, Rose Salzano, Theresa Garvey, Johanna McManus, and teacher Miss Smith.

MARLBORO UNION FREE SCHOOL GIRLS BASKETBALL TEAM, 1931. This basketball team included, from left to right, (first row) Jenny Kettenburg, Dot Conn (captain), Hetty Conner, and Edith Quimby; (second row) Ruth Baxter, Roberta Baxter, Ruth Staples, Mary Batten, Coach Butterfield, Dot Doscher, Virginia Herberich, and Mary Marrow.

MARLBORO UNION FREE SCHOOL GIRLS BASKETBALL TEAM, 1932–1933. This photograph, donated by Virginia Herberich McCourt, includes, from left to right, (first row) Mary Quintilliani, Louise Quintilliani, Mary Batten, Chris Chillura, and Lucille Morrow; (second row) Vincy Pagano, Frances Suffern, Virginia Herberich, Annie Erceg, Mary Morrow, Rose Pagano, and coach Ronald Long.

Marlboro Union Free School Girls Basketball Team, 1929–1930. This team included, from left to right, (first row) Mary Batten, Caroline McMullen, Jenny Mondello, and Mary Marrow; (second row) Coach Butterfield, Constance Ferguson, Naomi Staples, unidentified, Edith Quimby, Heddie Gallagher, and Principal Carroll Kearny.

Marlboro Union Free School Boys Basketball Team, 1929–1930. This team included, from left to right, (first row) Sam Zambito, Jack Tudico, and Raymond "Bunny" Frazier; (second row) Coach Butterfield, Alton Sarles, Sterling Elison, Mark Batten, Leland Cassles, Cy Canzaneri, Tony Quintilliani, and Principal Carroll Kearney.

Marlboro Union Free School Boys Basketball Team, 1931–1932. Posing for this team photograph are, from left to right, (first row) Jasper Canzaneri, Jake Alonge, Tony Quintilliani, Joseph Garcia, Olinto Fregerio, and Ignazio Zambito; (second row) Walter Smith, Principal Carroll Kearney, Charles Gaffney, Raymond Frazier, Jack Tudico, Cy Canzaneri, Sal Dragotta, and Kenneth Mabee.

Marlboro Union Free School Boys Basketball Team, 1932–1933. This team included, from left to right, (first row) Sid LoBurgio, Jake Alonge, Joseph Garcia, Olinto Fregerio, Jasper Canzaneri, and manager Ignazio Zambito; (second row) Jake Cutrone, Tony Quintilliani, Cy Canzaneri, Clifton Cassles, Charles Gaffney, Raymond Frasier, and coach Ronald Long.

Marlboro Central High School. Currently the Marlboro Middle School, this building at 1375 Route 9W was constructed in 1936 as the first Marlboro Central High School. On July 1, 1936, the Marlboro Union Free School ceased to exist. The new Central District No. 1, which included Milton, West Marlboro, Lattintown, and Mount Zion, came into being. The class of 1937 was the first graduating class from the new Central District. This photograph is from the Mannese/Panzella Collection.

Milton Elementary School. According to *Schools of the Town of Marlborough*, before 1935, "Milton had discussed buying property for a school, but the voters took no action. Building of two new schools for Marlboro and Milton was only possible if the districts were centralized. The Department of Education recommended that the Public Works Administration grant funds to a possible central district for the grade and high school building. A special school meeting was held on October 15, 1935 in Saint James Hall, Milton, to vote on the question of centralization. Of 571 votes cast, 418 voters favored centralization, 148 were opposed, and five ballots were left blank. In November of 1935, the school voters agreed to build the two schools, which with the Lattintown School, would make up the school district at that time." This photograph of the original school building, completed in 1936, shows the front facing Milton Turnpike with Route 9W in the background. This photograph is from the Dalby/Lyons Collection.

Marlboro Honor Roll. This wooden monument was erected to honor those who entered into military service from Marlborough. It was on the lawn of Marlboro Middle School facing Route 9W since the 1980s. A more permanent stone memorial honoring all those who served in various wars and conflicts replaced this wooden honor roll in 1988. This photograph is from the Mannese/Panzella Collection.

Marlboro Central High School Boys Baseball Team, 1945. This baseball team included, from left to right, (first row) Albert Shortt, Jim Marsiglio, Myles Doyle, and Michael LaPolla; (second row) Ralph Lofaro, Ed Brown, Charlie Ryerson, Frank Biasini, and Vincent Calabaro; (third row) Anthony Panduseo, John Minadeo, Bob Kenny, Burton Harris, John Nicklin, and unidentified; (fourth row) Edward Rhodes, Pete Chando, Art McDonald, Jim Zuentillino, Michael Pagano, Rick Malia, Jack Michaelson, and coach Fritz Becker. This photograph is from the Dalby/Lyons Collection.

MARLBORO CENTRAL HIGH SCHOOL, CLASS OF 1944. The name identifications on this photograph have been made by Harold Velie. The graduating class included, from left to right, (first row) Blanch Kramer, Mary Bond, Adele Sanders, Marie Schlesinger, Patricia Walmsley, Mary Zambito, Barbara Armstrong, Rose Canosa, Rose Diorio, and Florence DeCunzo; (second row) Theresa Rodelli, Anna Goodfriend, Grace Festa, Cornelia Partington, Mary Dragotta, Betty Northrip, Doris Polizzi, and Eleanor Decker; (third row) Anna Ferrara, Alice Ryan, Henry Alford, Ernest Borchert, Harold Velie, Francis Flannery, Bob J. LaPolla, Anne Pascale, and Phyllis Palmer; (fourth row) George Churchill, Anthony Russo, Bob A. LaPolla, John Gow, Charlie Glancy, "Ned" McNicholas, Vincent Ianuzzi, and Dick Barley.

MARLBORO UNION FREE SCHOOL, 1920. The students and faculty of this Grand Street school posed for this photograph on the southern side of the school facing Church Street. They are, from left to right, (first row) Helen Berkery, Catherine Dowd, Evelyn Clack, unidentified, Jack Benjamin, George Howard, Bill McGowan, Gus Wischoff, Ed Mills, George Suiter, Stanley Reynolds, and Andy Masca; (second row) Mande Kniffin, ? Santinello, Evelyn Tuthill, Viola Staples, Cornelia Atkins, James Brogan, Kenneth Mabee, John Bingham, Doc Rusk, Charles Bingham, Herbert Conn, John Manion, Frank Colletti, Edmund Nicklin, and James Cooney; (third row) unidentified, Miss Quinterra, Mary Clifford, Agnes Denmin, Margaret Kaley, Marian Barry, Loretta Berkery, Grace Vandersort, Jennie Perkins, Alice DuBois, Winifred McManus, Helen Staples, Florence Bingham, Grace Hedin, Margaret Berkery, Evelyn Clark, Clara Anderson, and Helena Hedin. Principal David D. Taylor stands in the middle behind the third row.

Marlboro Central High School Girls Leaders Club, 1944–1945. This photograph includes, from left to right, (first row) Marie Pucsio, Phylis Merrit, and Charlotte Wygant; (second row) Doris Dalby, Jacqueline Palmer, Shirley Nicklin, Jonn Cosman, and Miss Brescetti; (third row) Isabelle Kiss, Mildred Carden, Gloria Clarke, Berty Lyons, and Irene Stolfe. This photograph is from the Dalby/Lyons Collection.

Marlboro Central High School Boys Basketball Team, 1944–1945. This team included, from left to right, (first row) Ed Brown, Rick Malia, John Minadeo, Frank Biasine, and Nelson Dena; (second row) Frank Taorminia, Michael Pagano, Peter Mannese, and Jim Quintilliano; (third row) coach Fritz Becker, Angelo Foglio, Louis Sarinksy, and Vincent Mannese. This photograph is from the Dalby/Lyons Collection.

Marlboro Elementary School. Located near the intersection of Young Avenue and Route 9W, this photograph shows the school under construction in July 1960. It is directly across the street from today's Marlboro Middle School. Additions and upgrades were made to the school in 2005. Marlboro Elementary School celebrated its 50-year anniversary in 2010.

Dedication

June 1968

Each community builds a monument symbolic of an ideal cherished by its people. The voters and taxpayers of the Marlboro Central School District have chosen to build a magnificent one, representative of their concern for education. You have chosen to build a school and in so doing, have shown your hope for the future and faith in your youth.

Let us, in turn, aspire to greater heights because of your faith. May your pride in us grow.

For the Senior Class, for all of the students in the school system now, and for those to come, we wish to express our sincere gratitude by dedicating this yearbook to you—the community.

The Class of '68

Marlboro Central High School. This dedication spread from the 1968 class yearbook depicts ongoing construction of the new building erected on Cross Road in Marlboro. The class of 1968 was the first to graduate from this new high school. The original high school building constructed on Route 9W in 1937 has served as a middle school since the completion of the Cross Road building.

Eight

The Fire Departments

CONSTITUTION
AND BY-LAWS
OF

Marlboro Hose Co. No. 1
of Marlborough, New York

Organized May, 1895 Incorporated March 17. 1897

Constitution and Bylaws Booklet. This original booklet of the Marlboro Hose Co. No. 1 was donated to the Marlboro Free Library local history collection from the Will Plank Museum of Marlboro. The Marlboro Hose Company was organized in May 1895 and incorporated in March 1897. This booklet was published in 1917 by the Record Press in Marlboro.

Marlboro Hose Co. No. 1. The fire department was on Main Street (Route 9W) north of McMullen's Hotel. This photograph shows, from left to right, (children in the first row) George Masten, Bill Newman, Herbert McMullen, Ed Mullnix, Fred Crook, and Bert Kniffen; (second row) Lynk Dewitt and Elmer Yeaple; (third row) Tom Gregg, Charles Brown, Doyley Hutchins, Dimmick Bloomer, Ike Kniffen, Frank Richardson, Nattie Morgan, Pete Jackson, Speck White, Frank DuBois, Nat Jackson, Ted Covert, Mike Casey, Sidney McMullen, Lindsey Hutchins, Pat Gallagher, Howard "Toot" Kniffen, Harry McLean, and Ed Bradley. This photograph is from the Manion Collection.

Marlboro Hose Company, 1920s. The fire department is gathered here in uniform on King Street near the intersection of Western Avenue. Two local businesses of the time, Chas. Lester Plumbing & Heating and McGowan's Hotel, are in the background. The photograph is from the Badner Collection.

American LaFrance Fire Truck, Marlboro. Retired firefighter Doyley Hutchins sits in the American LaFrance fire truck on Western Avenue in 1950. Purchased by the Marlboro Hose Company in 1924, it was soon used to quell a fire that started early Christmas morning on the Carpenter block in the village. This photograph is from the Panzella/Mannese collection.

Western Avenue Firehouse, Marlboro. The Marlboro firehouse at 24 Western Avenue is seen here under construction in 1950. This firehouse served the community until 1976, when the village built a larger firehouse that still stands on the corner of Church and Grand Streets on the former site of the old Marlboro Union Free School. The photograph is from the Panzella/Mannese Collection.

MARLBORO HOSE COMPANY LADIES AUXILIARY, C. 1970. These auxiliary ladies are, from left to right, Grace McMullen, Peg Wischoff, Thelma Atkins, Mary Stant, Callie Atkins, Antonette McMullen, and Sis Partington. The Marlboro Hose Co. No. 1 Ladies Auxiliary was formed in 1954. This photograph was donated by Joan Diorio.

MARLBORO FIRE DEPARTMENT. This young girl poses in front of a fire truck. According to Plank, "Each year school children from the Marlboro Elementary School visit the fire trucks and firehouse during fire prevention week."

MILTON FIRE DEPARTMENT. The Milton Engine Company was organized on May 27, 1904. The original firehouse was a carriage house on Dock Road. In 1911, it was moved to a bank building on Main Street in Milton. The first piece of fire apparatus was a Gleason and Bailey hand pumper, which Jack Benjamin Sr. stands next to. This photograph is from the Panzella/Mannese Collection.

MILTON FIREHOUSE. Construction of the Milton fire station on Main Street began in 1951. The fire company also purchased a new Sanford fire truck at that time. That building still serves the community today, with a second floor added in 1967. This photograph is from the Panzella/Mannese Collection.

MILTON ENGINE CO. NO. 1. Posing in front of the current firehouse are members, from left to right, (first row, kneeling) Joseph Rodelli and Jim Timperio; (second row, seated) Edgar Rhoades, Sonny Rhodes, Thomas Govin, Carl Rhodes, Danny Diorio, Michael Rodelli Sr., James Conklin, Jim Appler, and Jason Martin; (third row) Oliver P. Kent, Marshall Rodelli Jr., John Matthews, John Dagastino, Sam Diorio, Russell Curtis, Frank Santora, Frank LoFaro, Ray Tabasco, Joseph Galente, and Charles Smith; (fourth row) Joseph Porpiglia, Joseph Dirago, Larry Diorio, Thomas Jenkins, Ralph LoFaro, Charles Weed, James VanVliet Jr., Michael Mataraza, Michael Rodelli Jr., two unidentified men, and Charles Mataraza. (From *Milton Engine Co. No. 1: One Hundred Years of Protecting With Pride*).

Roll Call

We the undersigned hereby orga-
nize the Milton Fire Engine associati[on]
No 1 of Milton N.Y Dated at Milton N.Y
this 24th Day of May 1904

E. F. Patten
C. J. Miller

1 Philip A Lyons 1111
2 E F Patten 0000
3 C J Miller 0000
4 Edward Young 1110
5 Fred Miller 0000
6 Hugh V. Briscoe 1111
7 Garrie Hornbeck 1000
8 Edward Ennest 1101
9 James Butler 0111
10 Ennis Hulse 1000
11 E R Walde 0000
12 William L De Witt 0101
13 Fred H Smyth 0011
14 A J Booth Jr 1100
15 J J Kaley 0000
16 William Butler 1001
17 Jeremiah A Driscoll 0011
18 C E Rice 0001
19 John B Ball 0101
20 I S Ferguson 0001
21 Arthur E Bell 0000
22 Geo Mertes 0000
23 H H Hallock 1100
24 D J Freston 0000
25 C P Braine 0000
26 F L Wood 0000

Original Roll Call for Milton Fire Co. No. 1. This document is dated May 24, 1904. The original fire department members listed on it are Philip A. Lyon, E.F. Patten, C.J. Miller, Edward Young, Fred Miller, Hugh V. Briscoe, Garry Hornbeck, Edward Ennest, James Butler, Ennis Hulse, E.R. Walde, William L. Dewitt, Fred H. Smith, A.J. Booth, John Joseph Kaley, William Butler, Jeremiah A. Driscoll, C.E. Rice, John B. Ball, I.S. Ferguson, Arthur Bell, George Mertes, H.H. Hallock, D.J. Freston, C.P. Brine, and F.L. Wood. This souvenir booklet was donated to the Marlboro Library by Gael R. Appler Jr. (From *Milton Engine Co. No. 1: One Hundred Years of Protecting with Pride.*)

Nine

Historical Buildings and Community

Old Dwelling, Milton. This house was built by John Young before 1760. According to Woolsey, "In December 1760, Edward Hallock, father-in-law of John Young, moved his entire family from Long Island to this small home. Nineteen people in all lived in the house during the winter of 1760."

ANNING SMITH HOMESTEAD, MILTON. This historic house is on the Barbarie Patent in the northernmost part of the Town of Marlborough. The Smiths moved to Milton from Long Island around 1762 and the house was built some time soon after. According to Woolsey, "Anning Smith served as a lieutenant in the William Gross Company of Colonel Johannes Jensen's Regiment of New York during the American Revolution." In 1953 and 1954, the house was owned by opera singer Dorothy Maynor, the first African American and the first woman to sit on the board the Metropolitan Opera in New York City. The house is now part of Buttermilk Falls Bed and Breakfast. (Courtesy of Joanne Pagnotta.)

Hallock House, Milton. This homestead on the east side of Route 9W is the oldest house still standing in Marlborough. Built around 1760, it is now part of the Kent property. During the American Revolution, the house was fired upon by Gen. John Vaughn's ship as it sailed up the Hudson River to burn the city of Kingston. (Courtesy of Joanne Pagnotta.)

Lewis DuBois House, Marlboro. This home was constructed between 1751 and 1765 and was the first clapboard house built in Ulster County. It was also fired upon by Gen. John Vaughn's forces as they made their way up the Hudson River during the Revolutionary War. The house was not hit, but several cannonballs were found later around the house. The house is now owned by Marie and George Rusk.

Elijah Lewis House, Milton. The land on which the Lewis House was built was part of the original Bond Patent. According a 1973 write-up by Sorens K. Peterson titled "The Old Spy House," "no doubt George Washington, on his travels along the Hudson, stopped at the old house often, as it was occupied as a tavern during the Revolutionary War, and known as headquarters for the spies of the Continental Army. The tavern owner, who answered to the name of Elijah Lewis, also ran a ferry across the Hudson." Harriet Hulse bequeathed the house to Mr. and Mrs. Arnold Zellner. The barn, which still stands on the property, was used for several years by the famous Hudson River School artist George Inness. (Courtesy of Bob Zellner.)

The William Cromwell Young House, Marlboro. Alexander and John Young came to Milton around 1760. John's son, William C. Young, then bought property in Marlboro and built a house. This property included the large Young's Farm, Young's Camp, and Young's Dock. Located on the east side of Route 9W east of the Marlboro Elementary School, the home is now owned by the Harry Lyons Sr. family.

The Elliot-Buckley House, Marlboro. The Elliot-Buckley House on Old Post Road in Marlboro was placed in the National Register of Historic Places in 2011. According to the home's website, "the house was built in federal style about 1843 by Dr. Daniel Elliot." In 1959, the house was sold to Romuald and Sharon Lanthier, who sold it to Richard and Claudette Hennessy in 1972.

Buckley Bridge, Marlboro. Located on Old Post Road, this bridge crosses Jews Creek in the southernmost part of Marlborough. It was destroyed by a vehicle in 2007, but has since been repaired to its former beauty. This photograph is from the Goudy Collection.

Independent Order of Odd Fellows. The Odd Fellows Advance Lodge No. 490 was instituted on January 18, 1882, in Marlboro. It met on Wednesday evenings in the Odd Fellows Hall in the Hartshorn Building on Route 9W. Here, the lodge members are gathered for a photograph in the early 1900s.

Shady Brook Farm Bed and Breakfast, Marlboro. This historic landmark at 183 Old Post Road was built before 1850. The Caywood family is first mentioned on the deed of 1878. A.J. Caywood and Sons became known for several varieties of grapes. The Caywoods also established the Shady Brook Farms boardinghouse, which welcomed summer visitors for many years. In the early 1930s, American impressionist Alfred Maurer spent several summers in a cottage behind the main house and painted many scenes of the Hudson Valley. Frances Perkins, the secretary of labor under Pres. Franklin D. Roosevelt in the 1930s, and her family also vacationed at Shady Brook Farm. (Courtesy of Maurice and Mary Menasche.)

Old Carlton Inn, Milton. This house was built by Nathaniel Hallock in the early 1800s at the junction of Old Route 9W and Willow Tree Road. It was the birthplace of Mary Hallock Foote, the author and illustrator and niece of Sarah Hull Hallock, who had been a strong supporter of the civil rights movement and women's suffrage. Susan B. Anthony and Frederick Douglass were welcome visitors at the home. Years later, this home became known as the Carlton Inn after another visitor, Irish author William Carlton. (Courtesy of Joanne Pagnotta.)

DuBois/Sarles Octagon House, Marlboro. This 19th-century octagon house with a mansard roof is on the bluff on the west side of Route 9W in the village of Marlboro. The house was built by General DuBois in the early 1850s. Beginning in 1872, it was owned by Benjamin Sarles and stayed in the Sarles family for many years. It is now owned by the Elizondo/Clouse family. It was placed in the National Register of Historic Places on November 12, 2002.

ELVERHOJ ART COLONY. According to Plank, "Few people realize that one of the first summer theatres that has since become so popular was established at the Elverhoj Art Colony on the river, nears the old Sears dock, between Marlboro and Milton. Originally designed as a summer retreat and workshop for the arts and crafts, Elverhoj later had a beautiful Moorish terrace overlooking the river, which became a popular restaurant and nightclub. Father Divine bought the property in the 1930s."

WILL PLANK, 1969. According to the February 17, 1976, *Southern Ulster Times* article "Will Plank Travels On" by Patricia Argiro, "Will Plank first came to Marlboro in 1921. He purchased the *Marlboro Record*, and then branched out with a chain of four weekly newspapers serving most of Southern Ulster County." He also founded the *Southern Ulster Pioneer*. Plank was the author of the Civil War history book *Banners and Bugles* and the 1959 book *The History of Marlborough*. Plank also had the Plank Historical Museum in his home on Hudson Terrace in Marlboro, which housed many local history and Civil War artifacts. He married Elizabeth Hendee in 1924, and he died in 1976.

Hallock Homestead, Milton. This house on Watson Avenue in the hamlet of Milton was built by George Hallock in 1862. Hallock owned a cider and gristmill adjacent to the house. Soldiers returning home from the Civil War were paid to help build the house. The home sits on 25 acres of Hallock family property. (Courtesy of Glenn Clarke.)

Marlboro-Milton Lions Club. In recognition of the United States' bicentennial celebration, the Marlboro-Milton Lions Club prepared a time capsule that was buried under the World War I monument in front of the old Marlboro Library on Kings Street. Standing next to the contents of the capsule are, from left to right, town historian John Matthews, Walter Kronner, and Thomas Amodeo.

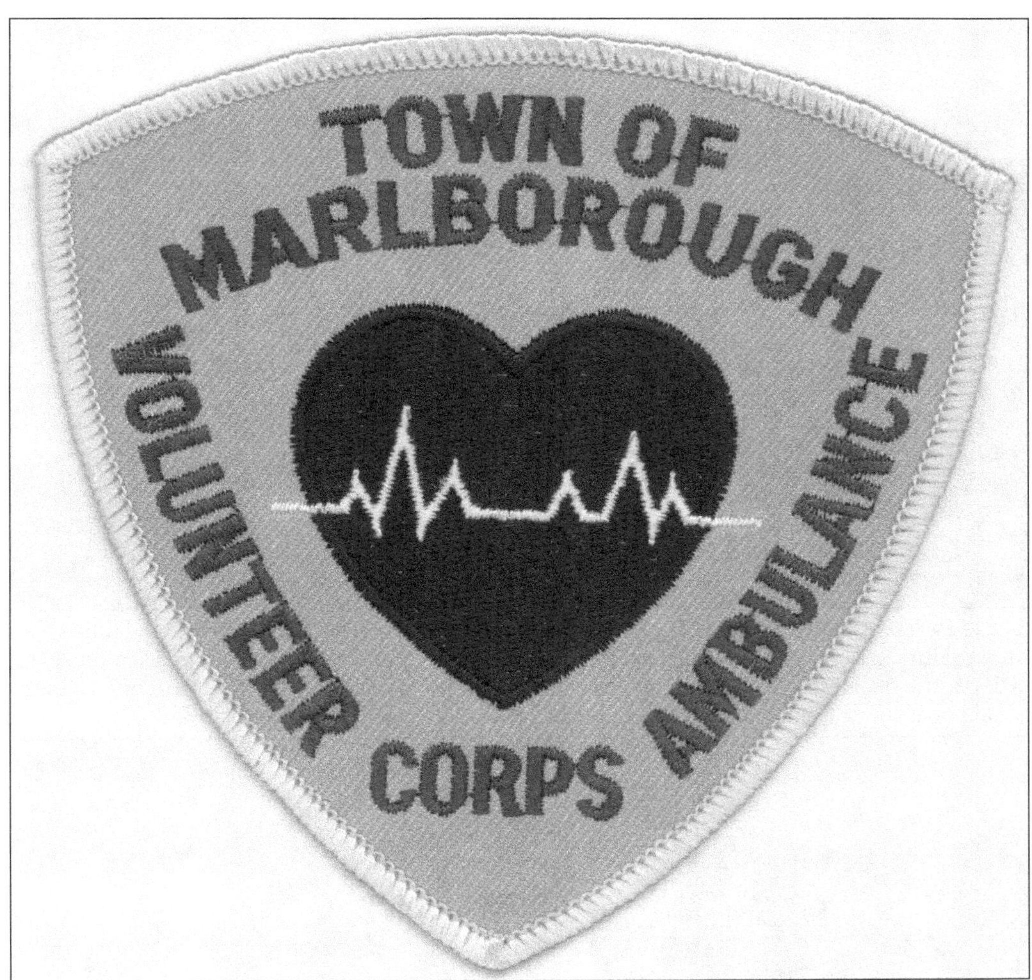

TOMVAC, Marlborough. The Town of Marlborough Volunteer Ambulance Corps (TOMVAC) was established in 1968 with the following charter members: Conrad Blom, vice president Joseph Canosa, Brenda Dall Vechia, Joaquin Delgado, Marilyn Delgado, Victoria Fridl, secretary Doris Hennekens, William Hennekens, Harold Herbert, William Jones, Jean Mazey, Grace McMullen, John Messina, Julies Miller, Mary Miller, Melanie Mower, treasurer Bernadette Polizzi, president Thomas Polizzi, Howard Quimby, Marie Renuad, Irene Russo, Vincent Russo, Carryl Vail, Ralph Walter, and Raymond Wenz. Honorary members were the Ralph C. Herman Company, Inc., and John J. McCourt, attorney-at-law. The TOMVAC celebrated its 25th anniversary on September 24, 1993, with an anniversary gala dinner dance. The organization ceased operations on January 13, 2009.

Sarles Building, Marlboro. Still standing on the southern corner of Bloom Street and Route 9W, this building has been a Methodist meetinghouse, an early Roman Catholic church, and starting in 1902, the business location of States Sarles Son, Inc., small engine repair. In this photograph, members of the Catholic church are gathered for a Christmas photograph in 1889.

Town of Marlborough Police Department, Late 1960s. The woman on the left is labeled as Helen "Daisy" Pascale, who served in the Women's Army Corps in World War II. Today, the Marlborough Police Department is located in the town hall, at 1650 Route 9W in Milton.

World War I Monument, Marlboro. This World War I honor roll is at the corner of King and Main Streets in front of the old Marlboro Free Library. The names listed on the monument are Antonio Amodeo, Bertha C. Baildon, John K. Baildon, James A. Barry, Victor M. Baxter, Walter H. Baxter, Walter S. Betts, Robert J. Canniff, John F. Casey, Benjamin Chillura, Gabriel Ciamihette, William H. Clark, William J. Conn, Melvin Coutant, Elting Crosby, James O. Crowley, Edward Dowling, Chester A. Gaede, Joseph W. Greaves, Ingham J. Grimley, Louise Haberle, C. Burton Harthorn, C. Gordon Hughes, Fred D. Hulse, Fred Kniffen, William Kniffen, Louis R. Lyons, Frank Lockwood, H. Worden Lockwood, Charles Marano, Vincent Marano, William H. Masten, Duncan Monroc, Edward McCarthy, Matthew McCourt, George McElrath, Edward McGowan, Joseph McGuire, John M. McLaughlin, Peter McMullen, Elmer Nelson, Harry Ogden, Clarence Polhamus, Allen H. Purdy, Orville J. Purdy, Harry Rhodes, Ruth Riggs, Constantine Robson, Charles E. Ryan, John Santinello, Ray L. Schoonmaker, J. Fred Schoonmaker, Alfred H. Shortt, Oscard A. Shortt, Abraham Smith, John Steffens, Louis E. Steinbach, Donald D. Strope, Frederick R. Strope, Charles D. Taylor, Perry Tschupp, Amodeo Valicenti, Anielle Vanacore, Burton Warren, George E. Warren, J. Calvin Wygant Jr., and Marion Wygant.

AMERICAN LEGION HALL, MARLBORO. The Viebey-Sutton Post No. 124 on Western Avenue, according to Plank, "Was organized in July 19, 1919 and was named after a sailor lost at sea. Young Viebey was Marlborough's first fallen military man. A fireman in the navy, his ship the *Mt. Vernon* was torpedoed in the English Channel in 1918." According to *Picture Book, As We Were—As We Are*, "In 1961, the post's name was changed to Viebey-Sutton. The names of Marlborough and Milton men who lost their lives in World War II were put into a box and town supervisor, John Quimby drew the name of Myron Sutton, who had been killed in Germany. The Legion Ladies' Auxiliary has been active for many years. The first president was Doris Polizzi in 1945. President during the opening year of the Bi-Centennial was Helen Pascale, who served four terms. She was succeeded in 1977 by Pearl Yeaple Smith."

GOMEZ MILL HOUSE, MARLBORO. The Gomez Foundation for Mill House interprets this historic site for four families who lived there throughout a 200-year period. The first was Luis Moses Gomez, a Sephardic Jew who traded with natives as early as 1714. The stream that flows through to the Hudson River is known as Jews Creek. This picturesque mill in the shape of an English country cottage complete with a thatched roof is a renovation of the original built by renowned craftsman and paper historian Dard Hunter.

Marlboro Boy Scouts. This group of Boy Scouts from the 1930s or early 1940s included, from left to right, (first row) Arthur Gow, William Conn, George Purdy, Myles Doyle, Louis Lyons, and Frank Bisini; (second row) Anthony Bucceri, John Gow, John Prizzia, Ryan ?, Barton Harris, and Scoutmaster John Gow; (third row) Harold Velie, Bill Stahl, Dick Barley, Chuck Walsh, Jerry Grasso, and Rusty Atkins. The photograph is from the Dalby/Lyons Collection.

Marlboro Girl Scouts. This photograph of the Marlboro Girl Scouts was taken during after the 1968 Memorial Day Parade. Ernestine Wygant helped start Girl Scouts in Marlboro in 1920, and in her old age, on May 31, 1997, she had a newspaper article written about her by Barbara Hart in the *Times Herald Record* titled "A Lifetime of Girl Scout Service: Marlboro Woman, 99, Inspires All Who Work to Preserve Group's History."

QUIMBY FAMILY CEMETERY. Sam Quimby kneels at the Quimby family plot on Mount Zion Road in Marlborough. Three members of the Quimby family have been supervisors of the town of Marlborough—Samuel L., Edward, and John Quimby—each one of whom lived in the house in the image below.

QUIMBY HOME, MARLBORO. This historic homestead on Ridge Road was built in 1840 by Matthew Harcourt. It consisted of two rooms with fireplaces and a loft above. Ownership passed to Dennis Purdy and, in 1885, to the Quimby family. Over the years, it has been enlarged to its present size, and it is currently occupied by Robert and Anne Quimby Cotton.

DiDonato Funeral Home, Marlboro. This home is in the middle of town on Route 9W. According to *Picture Book, As We Were—As We Are*, it was built "with the Mansard roof and Greek rival entrance. Mansard, who was a French architect, designed the flat roof to save on the roof tax." A. DuBois built the home in 1897, and it was once the home of H.S. Tuthill.

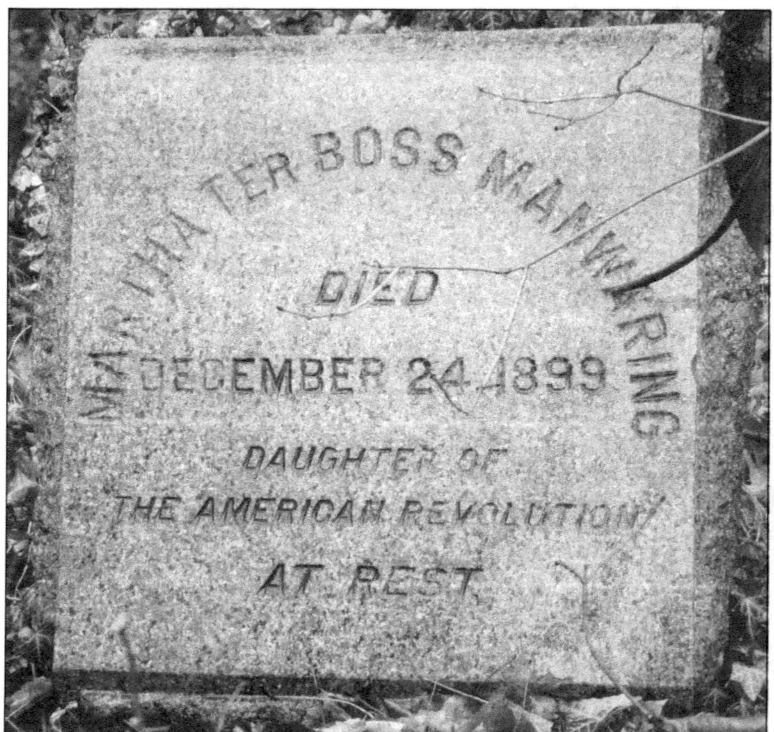

Original DAR Founder, Milton. The grave of one of the original founders of the Daughters of the American Revolution, Martha Ter Boss Manwaring, was found in the graveyard on the grounds of Milton Methodist Church.

Ten

Marlborough Notables of the Past

Frederic William Goudy. According to Plank, "This World-famous type designer was the best known resident of Marlborough, and did more to put the town on the map than any other individual." Goudy (1865–1947) designed seven types named after his Marlborough home, Deepdene, and two types named after Marlborough.

Deepdene, Marlboro. Frederic Goudy lived here from 1924 to 1947. According to Plank, "A fire one night in January 1939 destroyed his plant and the more than a century old mill, but Goudy continued to design and cut new faces of type for individual firms after that." According to *Picture Book, As We Were—As We Are*, Goudy and his wife, Bertha, "named their new home Deepdene after the one they had just left in Forest Hills, Queens, N.Y., on Deepdene Avenue."

Frederic Goudy Studio. Windows and skylights provided the type designer much-needed natural light. Goudy's type-designing workshop was located across the street from his Marlboro home on Old Post Road. It was, according to *Picture Book, As We Were—As We Are*, a "pre-Revolutionary War mill built in 1740, and held the Village Press, as well as his studio. The Village Letter Foundery stood on the floor below the studio."

Bertha M. Sprinks Goudy. Frederic W. Goudy maintained his foundry and press with his wife, Bertha (1869–1935). According to Plank, she was a "musician and lover of the arts. She helped her husband in his work and set type for some of his printing." They were both bookkeepers when they met. In Goudy's book, *Goudy's Type Designs: His Story and Specimens*, he writes, "As I worked, on the type design *Bertham*, the idea came to me that I might dedicate this 'one hundredth type' to my beloved helpmate, Bertha."

Frederic T. Goudy. Goudy also worked with his son Fred when casting type in his workshop. In the biography *Frederic Goudy*, D.J.R. Bruckner writes, "Being the only son of the two Goudys cannot have been easy. When Frederic T. was middle-aged his father was writing him, on hotel stationary, from California instructing him about how to build a new matrix-cutting machine. In a pamphlet addressed to Goudy in 1938, as part of the thirty-fifth anniversary of the Village Press, there are a couple of telling paragraphs from the son about the father. He wrote, 'I remember how greatly, when I was a small boy, you puzzled me. You worked harder than any of the [other fathers I'd seen], and longer." Fred Goudy is at right with his father and below with his wife, Alice.

George Inness Art Studio and Supply Box, 1889. George Inness (1825–1894) was an American Hudson River School landscape painter born in Newburgh. The above photograph shows the barn on the Zellner property on Old Indian Road in Milton that Inness used as an art studio for a period of time. The wooden supply box below, dated 1889, is believed to have belonged to the artist. (Both, courtesy of Bob Zellner.)

ALFRED MAURER. American artist Alfred Henry Maurer (1868–1932), according to Epstein's *Alfred H. Maurer: Aestheticism to Modernism*, "Began traveling to Shady Brook Boarding House on Old Post Road in Marlboro in 1915 or 1916, and continued to visit this retreat until the end of his life in 1932. Many of Maurer's landscapes painted after his return to the United States were made during his time at Shady Brook." Here, boarders relax on the lawn at Shady Brook around 1930.

SHADY BROOK, C. 1915. According to Stacy B. Epstein's *Alfred H. Maurer: Aestheticism to Modernism*, "Maurer, an extremely prolific painter, reportedly executed as many as two or three pictures a day during his stays in Marlboro. Maurer stayed at Shady Brook boarding house nearly every summer from May until October or November. Shady Brook provided Maurer with an ideal place to commune with nature." Seen here is the bridge and creek at Shady Brook, captured around the time Maurer vacationed there.

Dorothy Maynor. Opera singer and Milton resident Dorothy Maynor (1910–1996), the daughter of Rev. John J. Maynor and Alice Jeffries Maynor, was born on September 3, 1910, in Norfolk, Virginia. She began singing as a young girl in her father's church. She was educated at the Hampton Institute in Virginia and at Westminster Choir College in Princeton, New Jersey. In 1952, she was the first African American artist to perform at Constitution Hall in Washington, DC. (From the *Southern Ulster Times*.)

Maynor Residence, Milton. In 1961, Dorothy Maynor lived in the Anning Smith house, the current location of Buttermilk Falls Inn and Spa, at 220 North Road in Milton. She frequently dined with local residents at the Ship Lantern Inn. In 1963, she founded the Harlem School of Arts for young black artists. In 1975, she was the first African American to join the board of directors of the New York Metropolitan Opera.

Mary Hallock Foote. Writer and illustrator Mary Hallock Foote was born in the Hallock home at the corner of Willow Tree Road and Old Route 9W in Milton on November 9, 1847. She was the daughter of devout Quakers Anne Burling and Nathaniel Hallock. As a young girl, she attended the Female Collegiate Seminary in Poughkeepsie and then went on to be accepted at the Cooper Union in New York City.

Foote Sketch. In 1876, she married Arthur De Witt Foote and moved west, settling in the New Almaden area near San Jose, California. After sending illustrations of her surroundings to her friend Helena de Kay, de Kay's husband, Richard Watson Gilder, the editor of *Scribner's Monthly*, suggested she write stories to accompany her art, which he then published. The popularity of her stories were said to rival those of her contemporary Mark Twain.

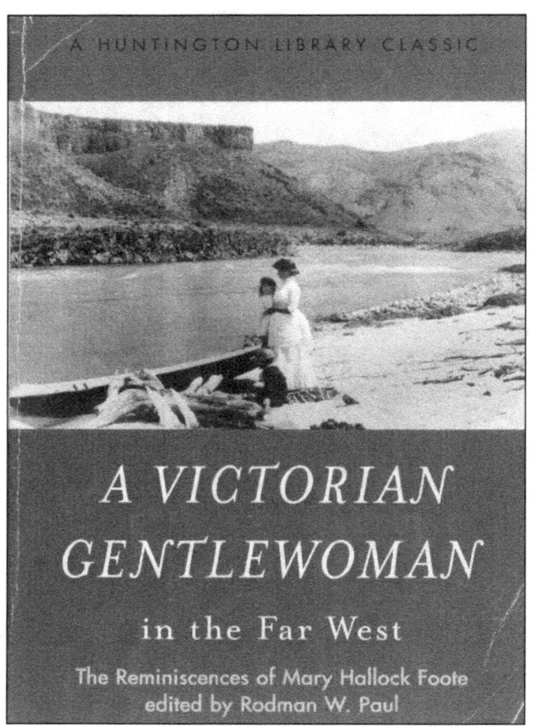

MARY HALLOCK FOOTE BOOK. Foote published eight books in her career, and two collections of stories were published after her death. The collection *A Victorian Gentlewoman in the Far West: The Reminiscences of Mary Hallock Foote* details her life in the west and also contains stories of her Quaker roots and happy memories of her early life in Milton.

JOHN BURROUGHS DESCENDANTS, 1913. Renowned literary naturalist and poet John Burroughs (1837–1921) taught at different locations in Marlboro and Milton in his early 20s. In his lifetime, Burroughs wrote more than 30 books and essays relating to nature. Seen here is the building that once stood at the current site of the Marlboro Library, on the corner of Route 9W and Bloom Street, where John Burroughs taught. His great-grandchildren and great-great grandchild are seated on the steps of the building. They are, from left to right, Joan Burroughs, Darcy Chamberlin, and Julia Burroughs.

Slabsides, West Park. In 1873, John Burroughs became a resident of West Park, New York, where he built a rustic cabin he named Slabsides in 1892. In the cabin, seen in both of these images, he wrote some of his famous nature books and entertained many famous visitors such as Thomas Edison, Henry Ford, and John Muir. The above postcard was sent to Mrs. J. Calvin Wygant of Marlboro from Elizabeth B. Kelley, the niece of John Burroughs. It is postmarked West Park, May 31, 1961, and was published by the Griffin Paper Company in Kingston. Today, Slabsides is maintained by the John Burroughs Society.

TONY CANZONERI. Professional boxing champion Tony Canzoneri is seen here in the 1920s in Marlboro. Canzoneri (1908–1959) bought a farm on Lattintown Road in Marlboro for his family. Antonino and Tony Canzoneri Jr. are listed among the original investors of the Marlboro Tomato Canning Factory. According to a local newspaper article dated October 7, 1927, "Tony Canzoneri, Marlborough featherweight, met Tommy Ryan of Buffalo in the ring at the Broadway Arena in Brooklyn. The boat was unusually one-sided. Ten rounds were fought, every one of which was given to Canzoneri. He knocked his opponent down three times. Ryan was not badly bruised, except about the face."

Edward Hallock Ketcham. Ketcham (1835–1864) was a lieutenant in the 120th New York Infantry in the Civil War. Ketcham enlisted at Kingston in August 1862 and died at the Battle of Gettysburg on July 2, 1863. He was buried in a field at Gettysburg, but his body was later exhumed and brought to Milton, where he was buried in the Hicksite Cemetery beside his brother, John Townsend Ketcham.

John Townsend Ketcham. Also a lieutenant, John Ketcham (1838–1863) was a member of the 4th New York Cavalry and enlisted in New York City on February 6, 1863. He was captured in a cavalry fight at Raccoon Ford, Virginia, and died in Libby Prison on October 8, 1863. He is buried in Milton.

Hicksite Cemetery, Milton. This small Quaker cemetery is on the west side of Route 9W at the junction of Willow Tree Road in Milton. It is the final resting place of brothers Edward Hallock Ketcham and John Townsend Ketcham, who lost their lives in the Civil War. Being of the Quaker faith, they were strongly opposed to war, but they had even stronger feelings about the abolition of slavery, so they chose to join the military and fight in the war. Augustine Joseph Hickey Duganne wrote a book about the Ketcham brothers titled *The Fighting Quakers: A True Story of the War for Our Union*. The book contains letters from the brothers to their mother.

Milton Art Colony and Scott Residence, 1959. According to Plank, artist James Scott "came to Milton with the Elverhoj Art Colony. His wife, Kirsten Scott was a gifted pianist and served as an accompanist for opera singer, Dorothy Maynor." The old Elverhoj Art Colony in Milton is seen above. Scott's former home (below) was featured in Marlborough's bicentennial picture book.

Bibliography

Bruckner, D.J.R. *Frederic Goudy*. New York City: Documents of American Design, H.N. Abrams, 1990.

Cochrane, Charles Henry. *The History of the Town of Marlborough, Ulster County, New York: From the First Settlement in 1712 by Cpt. Wm. Bond to 1887.* Marlborough, NY: 1887. Reprinted by Maryland Heritage Books, Inc., 1993.

Commemorative Biographical Record of Ulster County, New York: Biographical Sketches of Prominent and Representative Citizens and of Many of the Early Settled Families. Chicago: J.H. Beers & Co., 1896.

Epstein, Stacy B. *Alfred H. Maurer: Aestheticism to Modernism*. Essay. New York City: Hollis Taggart Galleries, 1999.

Foote, Mary Hallock. *A Victorian Gentlewoman in the Far West: The Reminiscences of Mary Hallock Foote*. Rodman W. Paul, ed. San Marino, CA: Huntington Library, 1992.

Goudy, Frederic W. *Goudy's Type Designs: His Story and Specimens: Being a Virtual Facsimile of the Typophiles Chapter Book XIII and VIV, A Half-Century of Type Design and Typography*. New Rochelle, NY: Myriade Press, 1978.

Hedrick, U.P., assisted by G.H. Howe, O.M. Taylor, Alwin Berger, G.L. Slate, and Olav Einset. *The Small Fruits of New York*. Albany, NY: J.B. Lyon Company, Printers, 1925.

Kanze, Edward. *The World of John Burroughs*. New York City: H.N. Abrams, 1993.

Mahan, MaryLou. *Marlborough on My Mind*. Bloomington, IN: iUniverse, 2009.

Matthews, John. *The History of Ulster County, New York: With Emphasis upon the Last 100 Years,1883–1983*. Kingston, NY: self-published, 1984.

McCausland, Elizabeth. *A.H. Maurer.* New York City: published for the Walker Art Center by A.A. Wyn, 1951.

One Hundred Years of Protecting with Pride. Milton: Milton Engine Company No. 1, 2004.

Petersen, Sorens K. "The Old Spy House." *The Hudson Valley* March 1973: 6, 7.

Plank, William. *History of the Town of Marlborough*. Marlborough, NY: The Fifty-Niner, 1959.

Schools of the Town of Marlborough. Marlborough, NY: Sponsored by the Parent-Teacher Associations of Marlborough, 1936.

Town of Marlborough Bi-Centennial Committee. *Picture Book, As We Were—As We Are*. Marlborough-Milton, NY: Hope Farm Press and Bookshop, 1978.

Woolsey, C.M. *History of the Town of Marlborough, Ulster County, New York: From its Earliest Discovery*. Albany, NY: J.B. Lyon Company, Printers, 1908.

Marlboro Free Library Local History Department. The authors of this book, local history researchers (from left to right) Emily Amodeo, James Cosgrove, and Joanne Sagarese Pagnotta, pose for a photograph in the Marlboro Library, of which Cosgrove is director. Together, they work to preserve the library's local history collection. The collection contains books, photographs, and other historical and genealogical materials, which are kept protected under lock and key. The library also has a digitized photograph and postcard collection online. The library's local history collection continues to grow thanks to donations made by the community over the years. (Photograph by Susan Scott.)